THE LITTLE

ZEN

COMPANION

THE LITTLE

ZEN

COMPANION

◨

BY DAVID SCHILLER

WORKMAN PUBLISHING · NEW YORK

LIBRARY OF CONGRESS CATALOGING-IN-PUBLICATION DATA

THE LITTLE ZEN COMPANION BY DAVID SCHILLER.
ISBN 1-56305-467-1 (PBK.): $6.95
1. ZEN BUDDHISM—QUOTATIONS, MAXIMS, ETC.
2. ZEN MEDITATIONS.
BQ9267.L58 1994   294.3'443—DC20   92-50936
CIP

WORKMAN BOOKS ARE AVAILABLE AT SPECIAL DISCOUNTS
WHEN PURCHASED IN BULK FOR PREMIUMS AND SALES
PROMOTIONS AS WELL AS FOR FUNDRAISING OR
EDUCATIONAL USE. SPECIAL EDITIONS CAN ALSO BE CREATED
TO SPECIFICATION. FOR DETAILS, CONTACT THE SPECIAL
SALES DIRECTOR AT THE ADDRESS BELOW.

WORKMAN PUBLISHING COMPANY, INC.
708 BROADWAY, NEW YORK, NY 10003

MANUFACTURED IN THE UNITED STATES OF AMERICA
FIRST PRINTING MARCH 1994

10 9 8 7 6 5

FOR ASA,
AND ESPECIALLY FOR QUINN,
MY MASTER

◥

WITH SPECIAL THANKS TO
PETER, PAUL, RUTH, WAYNE,
AND TO BILL,
FOR HIS EXAMPLE

AN INTRODUCTION

Zen. The spare word holds a powerful attraction, perhaps as much because of what we don't know about it as what we do. People say "very Zen," and it seems to mean spiritual, uncluttered, calm, mystical and enigmatic—all at the same time. What is Zen? It might be easier to describe the sound of one hand clapping.

This book doesn't presume to define Zen, but instead to offer a taste of Zen's way of looking at the world: where the best moment is now, where things *are* what they seem to be, where we see with the refreshing directness of a child and not through eyes grown stale from routine. The sayings, poems, parables, stories and other words that follow have been chosen for their power to suggest, and also for the surprising pleasures of their language. Some are serious, some irreverent, some beautifully evocative. Some might be puzzling—when words are used not to communicate an idea, but as tools to plant a wordless truth, some pretty strange things can happen.

Collected here are words on the rigors of the Way, words that celebrate the ordinary, words on Masters and pupils, on nature and art, on the thingness of things and on the oneness of the universe, on the simple life, on enlightenment. Quite a few originated in the West. Henry David Thoreau may have lived in nineteenth-century New England, not medieval Japan, yet much of what he thought and wrote embodies the Zen spirit.

Start anywhere. Pick up the book in the beginning, the middle, the end. Read the entries all in a row or skip around. But give the words time to work. Meaning is not so immediately apparent, and many of the quotations will seem to change before becoming clear.

Of course, words can never be a substitute for experience. Reading about fruit just isn't the same thing as biting into a warm peach. But give the words time to work, and you might find—not the truth, but a glimpse.

A HISTORICAL NOTE

Zen began in China in the sixth century as a meeting of Indian Buddhism with Taoism, merging the speculative with the practical, the metaphysical with the earthy. Called *Ch'an* in China, it stressed meditation over teaching as the shortest, and steepest, way to realizing the Buddha-mind inherent in all of us. Two lines initially developed, the Northern school of gradual enlightenment and the Southern school of sudden enlightenment, with the Southern quickly becoming the dominant school. Zen reached its Golden Age in the T'ang and early Sung dynasties (roughly the seventh through the twelfth centuries) and arrived in Japan about 1190, where the houses of Soto and Rinzai continue to flourish. The first Zen teachers came to America around 1905.

In the beginner's mind there are many possibilities, but in the expert's mind there are few.

SHUNRYU SUZUKI

Before a person studies Zen, mountains are mountains and waters are waters; after a first glimpse into the truth of Zen, mountains are no longer mountains and waters are not waters; after enlightenment, mountains are once again mountains and waters once again waters.

ZEN SAYING

I'm not young enough to know everything.

J.M. BARRIE

The willow is green;
flowers are red.

ZEN SAYING

The flower is not red, nor is the willow green.

ZEN SAYING

Good pitching will always stop good hitting, and vice versa.

CASEY STENGEL

"**I** am going to pose a question," King Milinda said to Venerable Nagasena. "Can you answer?"

Nagasena said, "Please ask your question."

The king said, "I have already asked."

Nagasena said, "I have already answered."

The king said, "What did you answer?"

Nagasena said, "What did you ask?"

The king said, "I asked nothing."

Nagasena said, "I answered nothing."

"WHO'S ON FIRST" ZEN

If you have to ask what jazz is, you'll never know.

LOUIS ARMSTRONG

The tao that can be told
is not the eternal Tao.

The name that can be named
is not the eternal Name.

TAO TE CHING

After taking the high seat to preach to the assembly, Fa-yen raised his hand and pointed to the bamboo blinds. Two monks went over and rolled them up in the same way. Fa-yen said, "One gains, one loses."

ZEN KOAN

The thing about Zen is that it pushes contradictions to their ultimate limit where one has to choose between madness and innocence. And Zen suggests that we may be driving toward one or the other on a cosmic scale. Driving toward them because, one way or the other, as madmen or innocents, we are already there.

It might be good to open our eyes and *see*.

THOMAS MERTON

The Koan

Perhaps no aspect of Zen is as puzzling and yet intriguing to Westerners as the koan. Or as misunderstood. A koan is not a riddle, nor is it a paradox designed to shock the mind. Instead it is an integral part of a system honed over centuries to help bring the student to a direct realization of ultimate reality.

Taken from the Japanese *kō* ("public") and *an* ("proposition"), the koan can be a question, an excerpt from the sutras, an episode in the life of an ancient Master, a word exchanged in a mondo, or any other fragment of teaching. There are some 1,700 traditional koans in existence.

Koan practice begins when the Master assigns a classic first koan like *"Mu"*—Chao-chou's reply to the monk who asked him, "Has the dog Buddha-nature or not?" It may literally take years of living with *"Mu"* before a student truly understands it. But afterward, the next koans—and there may be as many as 500 of them, in five progressive stages—are often "answered" in rapid succession.

The great Japanese Master Hakuin wrote, "If you take up one koan and investigate it unceasingly, your mind will die and your will will be destroyed. It is as though a vast, empty abyss lay before you, with no place to set your hands and feet. You face death and your bosom feels as though it were on fire. Then suddenly you are one with the koan, and body and mind are cast off. . . . This is known as seeing into one's nature."

"But the Emperor has nothing on at all!" cried a little child.

HANS CHRISTIAN ANDERSEN

Wakuan complained when he saw a picture of bearded Bodhidharma, "Why hasn't that fellow a beard?"

Zen koan

Soon the child's clear eye is clouded over by ideas and opinions, preconceptions and abstractions. Simple free *being* becomes encrusted with the burdensome armor of the ego. Not until years later does an instinct come that a vital sense of mystery has been withdrawn. The sun glints through the pines, and the heart is pierced in a moment of beauty and strange pain, like a memory of paradise. After that day . . . we become seekers.

PETER MATTHIESSEN

One day a man approached Ikkyu and asked: "Master, will you please write for me some maxims of the highest wisdom?"

Ikkyu took his brush and wrote: "Attention."

"Is that all?" asked the man.

Ikkyu then wrote: "Attention. Attention."

"Well," said the man, "I really don't see much depth in what you have written."

Then Ikkyu wrote the same word three times: "Attention. Attention. Attention."

Half-angered, the man demanded: "What does that word 'Attention' mean, anyway?"

Ikkyu gently responded, "Attention means attention."

ZEN STORY

Standing on the bare ground . . . a mean egotism vanishes. I become a transparent eyeball; I am nothing; I see all; the currents of the Universal Being circulate through me; I am part or particle of God.

EMERSON

The nature of God is a circle of which the center is everywhere and the circumference is nowhere.

EMPEDOCLES

Every day people are straying away from church and going back to God.

LENNY BRUCE

Love God and do what you will.

St. Augustine

If the doors of perception were cleansed everything would appear to man as it is, infinite.

WILLIAM BLAKE

As I grew up I became increasingly interested in philosophy, of which they [his family] profoundly disapproved. Every time the subject came up they repeated with unfailing regularity, "What is mind? No matter. What is matter? Never mind." After some fifty or sixty repetitions, this remark ceased to amuse me.

BERTRAND RUSSELL

The eye with which I see God is the same eye with which God sees me.

MEISTER ECKHART

Fundamentally the marksman aims at himself.

ZEN IN THE ART OF ARCHERY

Ring the bells that still can ring.
Forget your perfect offering.
There is a crack in everything.
That's how the light gets in.

LEONARD COHEN

The gaps are the thing. The gaps are the spirit's one home, the altitudes and latitudes so dazzlingly spare and clean that the spirit can discover itself like a once-blind man unbound. The gaps are the clefts in the rock where you cower to see the back parts of God; they are the fissures between mountains and cells the wind lances through, the icy narrowing fiords splitting the cliffs of mystery. Go up into the gaps. If you can find them; they shift and vanish too. Stalk the gaps. Squeak into a gap in the soil, turn, and unlock—more than a maple—a universe.

ANNIE DILLARD

If you cannot find the truth right where you are, where else do you expect to find it?

DOGEN

The only Zen you find on the tops of mountains is the Zen you bring up there.

ROBERT M. PIRSIG

THE SECRET SITS

We dance around in a ring and
 suppose,
But the Secret sits in the middle
 and knows.

ROBERT FROST

What is Buddha?

Again and again students ask, "What is Buddha?" The Masters' seemingly nonsensical responses have survived over the centuries, often as koans.

What is Buddha?

"Three pounds of flax." TUNG-SHAN

"Dried shitstick." YUN-MEN

"This very mind." MA-TSU

"Not mind, not Buddha." MA-TSU

"What is not the Buddha?" NAN-YANG HUI-CHUNG

*"The cat is climbing up
the post."* PA-CHIAO HUI-CH'ING

"I never knew him." NAN-YANG HUI-CHUNG

*"Wait until there is one, for then
I will tell you."* NAN-YANG HUI-CHUNG

*"A new bride rides a donkey, the mother-in-
law leads it."* SHOU-SHAN

*"When you utter the name of Buddha, wash
out your mouth."* ZEN SAYING

"Look within, thou art *Buddha."*
THE VOICE OF THE SILENCE

The shell must be cracked apart if what is in it is to come out, for if you want the kernel you must break the shell. And therefore, if you want to discover nature's nakedness, you must destroy its symbols, and the farther you get in the nearer you come to its essence. When you come to the One that gathers all things up into itself, there your soul must stay.

MEISTER ECKHART

A Zen Vocabulary

KENSHO: self-realization; seeing into one's own nature

JIRIKI: "one's own power," referring to a person's endeavor to attain enlightenment through his or her own efforts

SATORI: a state of intuitive enlightenment, particularly the Enlightenment experienced by the Buddha

BODHISATTVA: an enlightened being who renounces entry into nirvana until all other beings are saved

Zen is the unsymbolization of the world.

R.H. BLYTH

Veronica: I saw somebody peeing in Jermyn Street the other day. I thought, is this the end of civilization as we know it? Or is it simply somebody peeing in Jermyn Street?

Alan Bennett

Rose is a rose is a rose is a rose.

GERTRUDE STEIN

Things are entirely
what they appear
to be and *behind them*
. . . there is nothing.

SARTRE

A monk once asked Yun-men, "What teaching goes beyond the buddhas and patriarchs?" Yun-men said, "Sesame cake."

Do you feel your hairs standing on end?

BLUE CLIFF RECORD

Once Ma-tsu and Pai-chang were walking along and they saw some wild ducks fly by.

"What is that?" the Master asked.

"Wild ducks," Pai-chang replied.

"Where have they gone?"

"They've flown away," Pai-chang said.

The Master then twisted Pai-chang's nose, and when Pai-chang cried out in pain, Ma-tsu said, "When have they ever flown away?"

ZEN KOAN

The fundamental delusion of humanity is to suppose that I am here and you are out there.

YASUTANI ROSHI

We see men haying far in the meadow, their heads waving like the grass they cut. In the distance, the wind seemed to bend all alike.

THOREAU

The raindrops patter on the basho leaf, but these are not tears of grief; this is only the anguish of him who is listening to them.

ZEN SAYING

Sometimes I go about in pity for myself,
    and all the while
A great wind is bearing me across the sky.

OJIBWA SAYING

There ain't no way to find out why a snorer can't hear himself snore.

MARK TWAIN,
Western koan

A monk asked Yueh-shan, "What does one think of while sitting?"

"One thinks of not-thinking," the Master replied.

"How does one think of not-thinking?" the monk asked.

"Without thinking," the Master said.

ZEN MONDO

Layman P'ang

A family man who rejected formal practice but sought enlightenment on his own, Layman P'ang (740–808/811) would inspire countless others through his devotion to the Way. One favorite story tells how the Layman freed himself from all possessions by loading them in a boat and sinking it in the middle of a river. Thereupon he and his daughter, Ling-chao, traveled from place to place as itinerant peddlers.

Layman P'ang seems to have known every major Zen figure of his time, studying with them and engaging them in dharma combat. Once, when questioned by Shih-tou about his life, the Layman offered the following verse:

> *My daily activities are not unusual,*
> *I'm just naturally in harmony with them.*
> *Grasping nothing, discarding nothing . . . .*
> *Supernatural power and marvelous activity—*
> *Drawing water and carrying firewood.*

He and Ling-chao spent their last two years living in a cave. One day the Layman announced that it was time to die and got himself fully prepared, asking his daughter to go outside and report when the sun reached noon. Instead she rushed back in and told him there was an eclipse. When the Layman went outside to see it, Ling-chao assumed her father's place and promptly died. "Her way was always swift," the Layman said, and waited a week to follow her.

A monk asked Chao-chou, "If a poor man comes, what should one give him?"

"He lacks nothing," answered the Master.

ZEN MONDO

Our life is frittered away by detail . . . Simplify, simplify.

THOREAU

Y‌ou are eight years old. It is Sunday evening. You have been granted an extra hour before bed.

The family is playing Monopoly. You have been told that you are big enough to join them.

You lose. You are losing continuously. Your stomach cramps with fear. Nearly all your possessions are gone. The money pile in front of you is almost gone. Your brothers are snatching all the houses from your streets. The last street is being sold. You have to give in. You have lost.

And suddenly you know that it is only a game. You jump up with joy and you knock the big lamp over. It falls on the floor and drags the teapot with it. The others are angry with you, but you laugh when you go upstairs.

You know you are nothing and know you have nothing. And you know that not-to-be and not-to-have give an immeasurable freedom.

JANWILLEM VAN DE WETERING

Life and love are life and love, a bunch of violets is a bunch of violets, and to drag in the idea of a point is to ruin everything. Live and let live, love and let love, flower and fade, and follow the natural curve, which flows on, pointless.

D.H. LAWRENCE

A morning-glory at my window
satisfies me more than the
metaphysics of books.

WALT WHITMAN

Lovely snowflakes, they fall nowhere else!

ZEN SAYING

Everything the same; everything distinct.

ZEN PROVERB

I have a commonplace book for facts, and another for poetry, but I find it difficult always to preserve the vague distinction which I had in mind, for the most interesting and beautiful facts are so much the more poetry and that is their success. They are translated from earth to heaven. I see that if my facts were sufficiently vital and significant—perhaps transmuted into the substance of the human mind—I should need but one book of poetry to contain them all.

THOREAU

When you are deluded and full of doubt, even a thousand books of scripture are not enough.

When you have realized understanding, even one word is too much.

FEN-YANG

The purpose of a fish trap is to catch fish, and when the fish are caught, the trap is forgotten.

The purpose of a rabbit snare is to catch rabbits. When the rabbits are caught, the snare is forgotten.

The purpose of words is to convey ideas. When the ideas are grasped, the words are forgotten.

Where can I find a man who has forgotten words? He is the one I would like to talk to.

CHUANG-TZU

If you meet on the way
 a man who knows,
Don't speak a word,
 —don't keep silent!

ZEN SAYING

The Buddha

Zen teems with odd answers to the question "What is Buddha?" "Who was the Buddha" is simpler. Born Siddhartha Guatama in the sixth century B.C.E in what is today Nepal, the Buddha was a wealthy prince of the Shakya clan. He married, had a son and lived a pampered life. His father carefully sheltered him from all misery. But during four excursions away from the palace he encountered four signs—an old man, a sick man, a corpse, and a monk. The first three symbolized humankind's suffering; the fourth, Siddhartha's destiny.

Siddhartha adopted the ascetic, homeless path, first with teachers and then, for nine years, on his own. But asceticism proved fruitless. He began to eat again—to formulate Buddhist ideas of the Middle

Path—and then settled under the famed bodhi tree, vowing to meditate until he solved the problem of suffering. Forty-nine days later he achieved his great Enlightenment as the Buddha—and the satori sought after by all Zennists. Reluctant even to speak of it because of its wordless nature, Siddhartha finally addressed a group of disciples, then gave his first discourse in the Deer Park in Benares and spent the rest of his long life teaching. He died at the age of eighty after eating spoiled food.

Buddha, as he became known, is not the only buddha. According to Buddhist writings there were six before him, and thirteen to follow. The next will be Maitreya, due to come in a future age and renew the dharma.

Ti-ts'ang asked Fa-yen, "Where are you going?"

Fa-yen said, "Around on pilgrimage."

Ti-ts'ang said, "What is the purpose of pilgrimage?"

Fa-yen said, "I don't know."

Ti-ts'ang said, "Not knowing is nearest."

ZEN MONDO

It is good to have an end to journey toward; but it is the journey that matters, in the end.

URSULA K. LE GUIN

If a man wishes to be sure of the road he treads on, he must close his eyes and walk in the dark.

St. John of the Cross

A monk asked Master Haryo, "What is the way?" Haryo said, "An open-eyed man falling into the well."

ZEN KOAN

Go—not knowing where.
Bring—not knowing what.
The path is long, the way
unknown.

RUSSIAN FAIRY TALE

The map is not the territory.

Alfred Korzbyski

The search is what anyone would undertake if he were not sunk in the everydayness of his own life. To become aware of the possibility of the search is to be onto something. Not to be onto something is to be in despair.

WALKER PERCY

If you seek, how is that different from pursuing sound and form? If you don't seek, how are you different from earth, wood or stone? You must seek without seeking.

WU-MEN

Where do we come from? What are we? Where are we going?

GAUGUIN,
inscription on one of his paintings

In walking, just walk. In sitting, just sit. Above all, don't wobble.

YUN-MEN

If you wish to drown,
do not torture yourself
with shallow water.

BULGARIAN PROVERB

A Zen Vocabulary

MUSHIN: no-mind, or detachment of mind; complete freedom from dualistic thinking

SAMADHI: collected concentration in which subject is no different from object

SHIKANTAZA: precisely sitting or meditating, with no supporting techniques such as counting breaths

MAKYO: a mysterious apparition, particularly a vision or dream arising out of meditation

ZENDO: a meditation hall

One cannot step twice into the same river.

HERAKLEITOS

Every exit is an entry somewhere else.

TOM STOPPARD

If all the waves of the
Zen stream were alike,
innumerable ordinary people
would get bogged down.

ZEN SAYING

The only joy in the world is to begin.

CESARE PAVESE

Another time I saw a child coming toward me holding a lighted torch in his hand. "Where have you brought the light from?" I asked him. He immediately blew it out, and said to me, "O Hasan, tell me where it is gone, and I will tell you whence I fetched it."

HASAN BASRI

What happens to the hole when the cheese is gone?

BERTOLT BRECHT,
Western koan

The Barbarian from the West

"Why did Bodhidharma come from the West?" is a familiar question in Zen literature. The reference is to an Indian Buddhist monk, Bodhidharma (c. 470–532), who traveled by boat from India to China during the sixth century and over time became known as the First Patriarch.

The story of Bodhidharma begins with his meeting the Emperor Wu, who assailed him with accounts of good Buddhist deeds and asked what merit he gained. "No merit," Bodhidharma replied. "Then what is the first principle of the Holy Teaching?" "Vast emptiness, nothing holy." "Who is confronting me?" the Emperor demanded. Bodhidharma said: "I don't know." From there Bodhidharma traveled north and meditated before a wall for nine years. (To keep from falling asleep, one legend has it, he cut off his eyelids; where they fell, tea plants grew, thus crediting him with bringing tea to China.) Before returning to India (or prior to dying in China by poisoning—accounts differ), Bodhidharma installed his student Hui-k'o as the Second Patriarch, and so the lineage began.

Though his teaching remained Indian in character, Bodhidharma is revered as the father of Zen and author of this classic verse defining its essence:

A special transmission outside the scriptures;
No dependence upon words and letters;
Direct pointing to the soul of man;
Seeing into one's nature and attaining
    Buddhahood.

If you want to understand Zen easily, just be mindless, wherever you are, twenty-four hours a day, until you spontaneously merge with the Way.

This is what an ancient worthy called "The mind not touching things, the steps not placed anywhere."

YING-AN

The true way goes over a rope which is not stretched at any great height but just above the ground. It seems more designed to make people stumble than to be walked upon.

FRANZ KAFKA

Easy is right. Begin right
And you are easy.
Continue easy and you are right.
The right way to go easy
Is to forget the right way
And forget that the going is easy.

CHUANG-TZU

The Great Way is not difficult
for those who have no preferences.
When love and hate are both absent
everything becomes clear and
      undisguised.
Make the smallest distinction
      however
and heaven and earth are set
      infinitely apart.

SENG-T'SAN

Comparisons are odious.

POPULAR FOURTEENTH-CENTURY SAYING

To set up what you like against what you dislike—this is the disease of the mind.

SENG-T'SAN

The Way is not difficult; only there must be no wanting or not wanting.

CHAO-CHOU

How shall I grasp it? Do not grasp it. That which remains when there is no more grasping is the Self.

PANCHADASI

Zen has nothing to grab on to. When people who study Zen don't see it, that is because they approach too eagerly.

YING-AN

Chi Hsing-tzu was raising a fighting cock for his lord. After ten days, the lord asked, "Is he ready?" Chi answered, "No, sir, he is still vain and flushed with rage." Ten days passed, and the prince asked about the cock. Chi said, "Not yet, sir. He is on the alert whenever he hears another cock crowing." When the prince's inquiry came again, Chi replied, "Not quite yet, sir. His sense of fighting is still smoldering within him." When another ten days elapsed, Chi said to the lord: "He is almost ready. Even when he hears another crowing, he shows no excitement. He now resembles one made of wood. His qualities are integrated. No cocks are his match—they will at once run away from him."

CHUANG-TZU

Zazen

At the heart of Zen practice is zazen, or "sitting" in "absorption." Though rooted in ancient meditative practices, zazen differs from other forms of meditation in that it uses no meditation object or abstract concept for the sitter to focus on. The aim of zazen is first to still the mind—the sitter's everyday monkey mind—and then, through years of practice, to reach a state of pure, thought-free wakefulness so that the mind can realize its own Buddhanature. And unlike other forms of meditation, zazen is not simply a means to an end. "Zazen is itself enlightenment," said Dogen. One minute of sitting, one minute of being a buddha.

The famous example of zazen is Bodhidharma, who sat for nine years facing a wall at Shao-lin monastery. But, typically, Zen literature yields an equally compelling example that appears to be its opposite. Day after day Ma-tsu sat in meditation, until his Master finally questioned him about it. Ma-tsu explained that he was hoping to attain Buddhahood. The Master picked up a piece of tile and began to rub it with a stone. When Ma-tsu asked him what he was doing, he replied that he was polishing the tile to make it a mirror. "How can you polish a tile into a mirror?" Ma-tsu asked. "How can one become a buddha by sitting in meditation?" the Master shot back—criticizing not the sitting, but the sitter.

And everything comes to One,
As we dance on, dance on, dance on.

THEODORE ROETHKE

Teach us to care and not to care
Teach us to sit still.

T.S. ELIOT

To be a man of knowledge one needs to be light and fluid.

YAQUI MYSTIC

Act without doing; work without effort.

TAO TE CHING

I take a nap
   making the mountain water
      pound the rice.

ISSA

We think in generalities, but we live in detail.

ALFRED NORTH WHITEHEAD

A Zen Vocabulary

DOKUSAN: a private meeting between student and Master in the seclusion of the Master's room; a key element of Rinzai Zen

ROSHI: a venerable teacher, whether a monk or layperson, woman or man

MONDO: a dialogue about Buddhism or an existential problem among Masters or between Master and student

INKA: a seal of enlightenment; a Master's official confirmation that a student has completed training

When the student
is ready, the Master
appears.

BUDDHIST PROVERB

Teachers open the door, but you must enter by yourself.

CHINESE PROVERB

Elder Ting asked Lin-chi, "Master, what is the great meaning of Buddha's teachings?"

Lin-chi came down from his seat, slapped Ting and pushed him away. Ting was stunned and stood motionless. A monk nearby said, "Ting, why do you not bow?" At that moment Ting attained great enlightenment.

ZEN KOAN

"Kwatsu!"

Zen is infamous for the unorthodox methods used by its Masters, particularly those of T'ang Dynasty China who developed Zen's "strange words and extraordinary actions" style of teaching. Yun-men answered his monks' queries with a single word. Ma-tsu knocked students to the ground, twisted their noses, and pioneered the use of the *shippei* (Japanese, *kyosaku*)—the "wake-up stick" used by meditation monitors.

Lin-chi perfected the *"Ho!"*—a sound that translates in Japanese as *kwatsu*, or just *kwats*, an exclamation used to shock students out of their dualistic thinking. Chao-chou's short, simple, paradoxical statements are unsurpassed for their inventiveness and form the basis of many koan.

And then there was the one-finger Zen of Chu-chih. One time an outsider asked Chu-chih's attendant what kind of Zen his Master preached. The boy held up just one finger, as did his Master when he was asked a question. On hearing of this, Chu-chih cut off the boy's finger with a knife. The boy began to run from the room, screaming with pain. Chu-chih called to him. The boy turned around. Chu-chih held up one finger. At that the boy was enlightened.

If you meet the buddha, kill the buddha.

LIN-CHI

Do not seek to follow in the footsteps of the men of old; seek what they sought.

BASHO

Somebody showed it to me and I found it by myself.

LEW WELCH

Why tell animals living in the water to drink?

WEST AFRICAN PROVERB

Farmer,
  pointing the way
    with a radish.

ISSA

You be Bosatsu,
  I'll be the taxi-driver
    Driving you home.

GARY SNYDER

Chiu-feng was an attendant of Shih-shuang, and when the Master passed away the community decided to invite the chief monk in the hall to succeed him. Chiu-feng did not agree. "Please wait until I question him. If he understands Shih-shuang's teaching, then I'll serve him like our late Master." Chiu-feng then turned to the chief monk. "Shih-shuang said, 'Cease, desist; spend ten thousand years in one thought; be cold ashes, dead trees; be a censer in an ancient shrine; be a strip of pure white silk.' Now tell me, which side does this illustrate?"

The chief monk said, "It illustrates the side of uniformity."

Chiu-feng said, "Then you still don't understand the late teacher's meaning."

The chief monk said, "If you don't agree with me, bring me a stick of incense." The chief monk then lit the incense and said, "If I do not understand the late teacher's meaning, then I won't be able to pass away while this incense is still burning." So saying he sat down and died.

Chiu-feng patted him on the back and said, "As far as dying seated or standing is concerned, you're not lacking. But as for our late teacher's meaning, you haven't even dreamed of seeing it."

ZEN STORY

113

In this very breath
that we take now lies
the secret that all great
teachers try to tell us.

PETER MATTHIESSEN

Zen is your everyday thought.

CHAO-CHOU

What is this true meditation? It is to make everything: coughing, swallowing, waving the arms, motion, stillness, words, action, the evil and the good, prosperity and shame, gain and loss, right and wrong, into one single koan.

HAKUIN

that stone Buddha deserves
    all the birdshit it gets
I wave my skinny arms like
    a tall flower in the wind

IKKYU

Water which is too pure has no fish.

Ts'ai Ken T'an

The one who is good at shooting does not hit the center of the target.

ZEN SAYING

The Sixth Patriarch

One day a poor, uneducated woodcutter named Hui-neng (638–713) overheard monks reciting a line from the Diamond Sutra—"Let your mind flow freely without dwelling on anything." It changed his life, and the history of Chinese Zen. Before his death Hui-neng, the Sixth Patriarch, would give Zen a wholly Chinese stamp by merging it with Taoist ideas (e.g., rejection of book learning) and, through his dharma successors, lead Zen into its Golden Age.

The watershed story about this great figure concerns his installment as the Sixth Patriarch. For eight months Hui-neng had toiled as a kitchen helper in a monastery when its leader, Hung-jen, the Fifth Patriarch, announced it was time to appoint a successor. Hung-jen asked the monks to write a

poem expressing their understanding of Zen.
The head monk, put this verse on a wall:

> *Our body is the bodhi* tree,*
> *And our mind a mirror bright.*
> *Carefully we wipe them hour by hour,*
> *And let no dust alight.*

Hui-neng dictated this version:

> *There is no bodhi tree,*
> *Nor stand of mirror bright.*
> *Since all is void,*
> *Where can the dust alight?*

Hung-jen knew at once who understood his teaching.

* The tree under which Buddha sat and attained enlightenment.

In dwelling, live close to the ground.
In thinking, keep to the simple.
In conflict, be fair and generous.
In governing, don't try to control.
In work, do what you enjoy.
In family life, be completely present.

TAO TE CHING

However innumerable sentient beings, I vow to save them all.

However inexhaustible the passions, I vow to extinguish them all.

However immeasurable the dharmas, I vow to master them all.

However incomparable the Buddha's truth, I vow to attain it.

THE FOUR VOWS

Where there are humans
   you'll find flies,
      and Buddhas.

ISSA

For everything that lives is
    holy, life delights in life.

WILLIAM BLAKE

A monk asked Yun-men, "What are the teachings of a lifetime?"

Yun-men said to him, "An appropriate statement."

ZEN MONDO

The Layman was once lying on his couch reading a sutra. A monk saw him and said: "Layman! You must maintain dignity when reading a sutra."

The Layman raised up one leg.

The monk had nothing to say.

One day the great Master Huang-po and a monk were walking along, talking and laughing together like old friends. When they came to a swollen river, the monk tried to take the Master across, but Huang-po said, "Please cross over yourself."

The monk walked across the waves as though walking on a level field. Once on the other side he called, "Come across! Come across!"

The Master scolded him: "You self-perfected fellow! If I had known you were going to perform a miracle, I would have broken your legs!"

The monk sighed with admiration and said, "You are a true Master of the Great Vehicle."

ZEN STORY

Unformed people delight in the gaudy and in novelty. Cooked people delight in the ordinary.

ZEN SAYING

When hungry, eat your rice; when tired, close your eyes. Fools may laugh at me, but wise men will know what I mean.

LIN-CHI

A Zen Vocabulary

DHARMA: cosmic law, secular law; the teaching of the Buddha; the Way; the general state of affairs. A central concept of Buddhism

KARMA: the Buddhist universal law of cause and effect

NIRVANA: the goal of Buddhism; freedom from karma; extinction of all craving; the realization of the true nature of the mind

TAO: the Way; the source of reality; the truth; the ultimate principle

Those who want
the fewest things are
nearest to the gods.

SOCRATES

I threw my cup away when I saw a child drinking from his hands at the trough.

DIOGENES

Sit
Rest
Work.

Alone with yourself,
Never weary.

On the edge of the forest
Live joyfully,
Without desire.

THE BUDDHA

This is what you shall do: Love the earth and sun and the animals, despise riches, give alms to everyone that asks, stand up for the stupid and crazy, devote your income and labor to others, hate tyrants, argue not concerning God ....

WALT WHITMAN

When the Many are reduced to One, to what is the One reduced?

ZEN KOAN

Among twenty snowy
     mountains
The only moving thing
Was the eye of the blackbird.

WALLACE STEVENS

Truly, I say to you, whosoever does not receive the Kingdom of God like a child shall not enter it.

LUKE 18:17

If my heart can become pure and simple like that of a child, I think there probably can be no greater happiness than this.

KITARO NISHIDA

Zen and the Art of Haiku

Haiku is the shortest form of poetry known in world literature, but its three little lines of 5-7-5 syllables are capable of expressing deep feeling and sudden flashes of intuition. There is no symbolism in haiku. It catches life as it flows. There is no egotism either; haiku is practically authorless. But in its preoccupation with the simple, seemingly trivial stuff of everyday life—a falling leaf, snow, a fly— haiku shows us how to see into the life of things and gain a glimpse of enlightenment. Haiku is not Zen, but Zen is haiku. It is, in the words of R.H. Blyth, "the final flower of all Eastern culture."

Haiku was elevated to its present form by the great poet Basho. Other poets include Buson, Issa, Ryokan, and Shiki. Like all Japanese arts that are

bound up with the spirit of Zen, haiku evokes *sabi*,
solitude, aloneness or detachment, and *wabi*, the
poignant spirit of poverty. Always, a season is men-
tioned—with plum blossoms for spring, for example,
the bare branches for fall. And like all the Zen arts,
haiku knows when enough has been said.

> *The butterfly*
> *Resting upon the temple bell,*
> *Asleep.*
>
> BUSON

Look, children,
 hail-stones!
  Let's rush out!

BASHO

TODAY.

WORD CARVED ON A STONE ON
JOHN RUSKIN'S DESK

It was evening all afternoon.
It was snowing
And it was going to snow.
The blackbird sat
In the cedar-limbs.

WALLACE STEVENS

Luis Ponce de León, returning to his university after five years' imprisonment by the Inquisition, resumed his lectures with the words: "As we were saying yesterday. . . ."

A man walking across a field encountered a tiger. He fled, the tiger chasing after him. Coming to a cliff, he caught hold of a wild vine and swung himself over the edge. The tiger sniffed at him from above. Terrified, the man looked down to where, far below, another tiger had come, waiting to eat him. Two mice, one white and one black, little by little began to gnaw away at the vine. The man saw a luscious strawberry near him. Grasping the vine with one hand, he plucked the strawberry with the other. How sweet it tasted!

ZEN PARABLE

Barn's burnt down—
now
 I can see the moon.

MASAHIDE

Every day is a good day.

Yun-Men

It loved to happen.

MARCUS AURELIUS

Thinking is more interesting than knowing, but less interesting than looking.

GOETHE

The whole of life lies in the verb *seeing*.

TEILHARD DE CHARDIN

One sees great things from the valley, only small things from the peak.

G.K. CHESTERTON

It is only with the heart that one can see rightly; what is essential is invisible to the eye.

ANTOINE DE SAINT-EXUPÉRY

We are more curious about the meaning of dreams than about things we see when awake.

DIOGENES

Once at Cold Mountain,
    troubles cease—
No more tangled, hung-up
    mind.
I idly scribble poems on the
    rock cliff,
Taking whatever comes,
    like a drifting boat.

HAN SHAN

Catch
   the vigorous horse
   of your mind.

ZEN SAYING

Let the nothingness into yer shots.

GOLF IN THE KINGDOM

When someone tosses you a
    tea bowl
  —Catch it!
Catch it nimbly with soft cotton
With the cotton of your skillful
        mind!

BANKEI

Whatever interests, is interesting.

WILLIAM HAZLITT

The melons look cool
  flecked with mud
    from the morning dew.

BASHO

Teach us to delight in simple
    things,
And mirth that has no bitter
    springs;
Forgiveness free of evil done,
And love to all men 'neath
    the sun.

RUDYARD KIPLING

Zen and the Art of Tea

Since the time of Bodhidharma, tea and Zen have been connected. Fittingly, it was one of Japan's first Zen Masters, Eisai, who brought tea seeds from China. And it was the Zen student Rikyu who refined the art of tea, *cha-no-yu*, in the sixteenth century.

Like Zen, the art of tea aims at simplification. It consists simply of boiling water, preparing tea and drinking it. Its spirit conjures up harmony, reverence, purity, tranquillity, poverty, solitariness; and it has deeply influenced the arts of flower arranging, pottery and architecture. The ceremony itself is practiced in a simple thatched hut—the "abode of vacancy." The utensils are few and unpretentious, and there is nothing else in the room except perhaps an arrangement of flowers or a single painting.

No more than four or five guests can be in the tea room, and they are welcomed by the singing of the kettle—pieces of iron are arranged inside it to create sounds that suggest a far-off waterfall or wind blowing through pines. An elaborate set of rules dictate how the thick green tea is whisked and served, how utensils should be passed and admired—all, paradoxically, to achieve tea's state of artless art.

Our Father which art in heaven
Stay there
And we will stay on earth
Which is sometimes so pretty.

JACQUES PRÉVERT

We gaze
  even at horses
    this morn of snow.

BASHO

God is in me or else is not at all.

WALLACE STEVENS

We consider bibles and religions divine—
   I do not say they are not divine,

I say they have all grown out of you, and
   may grow out of you still,

It is not they who give the life, it is you
   who give the life,

Leaves are no more shed from the trees,
   or trees from the earth, than they are
   shed out of you.

WALT WHITMAN

God is so omnipresent . . .
God is an angel in an angel,
and a stone in a stone, and a
straw in a straw.

JOHN DONNE

A hand-rolled
Dumpling of
Heaven-and-earth:
I've gulped it down
And easily it went.

DIM SUM ZEN

The squeaking of the pump sounds as necessary as the music of the spheres.

THOREAU

THE RED WHEELBARROW

so much depends
upon

a red wheel
barrow

glazed with rain
water

beside the white
chickens

WILLIAM CARLOS WILLIAMS

Do not, I beg you, look for anything behind phenomena. They are themselves their own lesson.

GOETHE

It is only shallow
people who do not
judge by appearances.

OSCAR WILDE

In so doing, use him as though you loved him.

ISAAC WALTON,
on baiting a frog

A Zen Vocabulary

PRAJNA: intuitive wisdom, insight into emptiness or the true nature of reality

SHUNYATA: emptiness or void, without essence; a key notion of Buddhism

HARA: belly or gut, which is a person's spiritual center

SAMSARA: succession of rebirths

HINAYANA: literally "Small Vehicle," the Northern Buddhist term for the Southern Buddhism of Southeast Asia

MAHAYANA: "Great Vehicle," the Northern Buddhism of China, Korea, and Japan

God made everything out of nothing. But the nothingness shows through.

PAUL VALÉRY

Picture a massless particle.

A KOAN OF MODERN PHYSICS

We shape clay into a pot,
but it is the emptiness inside
that holds whatever we want.

TAO TE CHING

The notes I handle no better than many pianists. But the pauses between the notes—ah, that is where the art resides!

ARTUR SCHNABEL

Even a good thing isn't as good as nothing.

ZEN SAYING

Among the great things which are to be found among us, the Being of Nothingness is the greatest.

LEONARDO DA VINCI

I have nothing to say, I am saying it, and that is poetry.

JOHN CAGE

You say my poems are poetry?
They are not.
Yet if you understand they are not—
Then you see the poetry of them.

RYOKAN

No one's mouth is big enough to utter the whole thing.

ALAN WATTS

Say one word
with your mouth shut!

ZEN SAYING

Enlightenment

Awakening—or satori, or kensho—is the fundamental aim of Zen. It is seeing into your nature, realizing your own Buddhahood, freeing yourself from the cycle of birth and death. It is "to die completely and then come back to life." According to the koan text *Denkoroku*, "Even if you sit until your seat breaks through . . . even if you are a person of lofty deeds and pure behavior, if you haven't reached satori you can't get out of the prison of the world."

Zen writing is filled with examples of unexpected things that trigger enlightenment—Buddha seeing the morning star, Bankei coughing up a blood clot, Hsiang-yen hearing a pebble strike a bamboo tree. But one of the best descriptions of the actual experience comes from the Master Sokei-an Sasaki:

"One day I wiped out all notions from my mind. I gave up all desire. I discarded all the words with which I thought and stayed in quietude. I felt a little queer—as if I were being carried into something, or as if I were touching some power unknown to me . . . and Ztt! I entered. I lost the boundary of my physical body. I had my skin, of course, but I felt I was standing in the center of the cosmos. I spoke, but my words had lost their meaning. I saw people coming toward me, but all were the same man. All were myself! I had never known this world. I had believed that I was created, but now I must change my opinion: I was never created; I was the cosmos; no individual Mr. Sasaki existed."

As regards the quietude of the sage, he is not quiet because quietness is said to be good. He is quiet because the multitude of things cannot disturb his quietude. When water is still, one's beard and eyebrows are reflected in it. A skilled carpenter uses it in a level to obtain a measurement. If still water is so clear, how much more are the mental faculties! The mind of a sage is the mirror of heaven and earth in which all things are reflected.

CHUANG-TZU

Enlightenment is like the moon reflected on the water. The moon does not get wet, nor is the water broken. Although its light is wide and great, the moon is reflected even in a puddle an inch wide. The whole moon and the entire sky are reflected in one dewdrop on the grass.

DOGEN

As the roof was leaking, a Zen Master told two monks to bring something to catch the water. One brought a tub, the other a basket. The first was severely reprimanded, the second highly praised.

ZEN KOAN

The bottom of a pail is broken through.

A ZEN MASTER,
on enlightenment

Even if our efforts of attention seem for years to be producing no result, one day a light that is in exact proportion to them will flood the soul.

SIMONE WEIL

Ten years' searching in
 the deep forest
Today great laughter at
 the edge of the lake.

SOEN

To study Buddhism is to study the self. To study the self is to forget the self. To forget the self is to be enlightened by all things. To be enlightened by all things is to drop off our own body and mind, and to drop off the bodies and minds of others. No trace of enlightenment remains, and this no-trace continues endlessly.

DOGEN

Anything more
than the truth
would be too much.

ROBERT FROST

At night, deep in the mountains,
I sit in meditation.
The affairs of men never reach here:
Everything is quiet and empty,
All the incense has been swallowed up
        by the endless night.
My robe has become a garment of dew.
Unable to sleep I walk out into the
        woods—
Suddenly, above the highest peak,
        the full moon appears.

RYOKAN

We must endure our thoughts
  all night, until
The bright obvious stands
  motionless in the cold.

WALLACE STEVENS

Crazy Cloud

An eccentric genius revered as much for his wit as for his understanding, Ikkyu Sojun (1394–1481) is a beloved figure in Japanese Zen. He was rumored to be the son of an emperor and lady-in-waiting. A brilliant child, he delighted in exposing the hypocrisy of the stultified and corrupt Zen of his era. Later, he sought out the most uncompromising teacher of his day. After years of pushing himself through severe training, he experienced a sudden enlightenment when, drifting in a boat across Lake Biwa at night, a crow raucously cawed.

After the death of his Master, Ikkyu wandered for the next thirty years, living among all segments of society—nobles, merchants, prostitutes, authors, and artists. He enjoyed the pleasures of women and sake, and continued to spit in the face of orthodoxy.

Ikkyu, who gave himself the name "Crazy Cloud," was an influential painter, calligrapher and poet. Two of his poems beloved by Zennists are:

VOID IN FORM

When, just as they are,
White dewdrops gather
On scarlet maple leaves,
Regard the scarlet beads!

FORM IN VOID

The tree is stripped,
All color, fragrance gone,
Yet already on the bough,
Uncaring spring!

We walk, and our religion is shown (even to the dullest and most insensitive person) in how we walk. Or to put it more accurately, living in this world means choosing, choosing to walk, and the way we choose to walk is infallibly and perfectly expressed in the walk itself. Nothing can disguise it. The walk of an ordinary man and of an enlightened man are as different as that of a snake and a giraffe.

R.H. BLYTH

The clearest way into the Universe is through a forest wilderness.

JOHN MUIR

Late on the third day, at the very moment when, at sunset, we were making our way through a herd of hippopotamuses, there flashed upon my mind, unforeseen and unsought, the phrase, "Reverence for Life."

ALBERT SCHWEITZER

The rocks are where they are—this is their will. The rivers flow—this is their will. The birds fly—this is their will. Human beings talk—this is their will. The seasons change, heaven sends down rain or snow, the earth occasionally shakes, the waves roll, the stars shine—each of them follows its own will. To be is to will and so is to become.

D.T. SUZUKI

What's this little brown insect
  walking zigzag
across the sunny white page of
  Su Tung-p'o's poem?
Fly away, tiny mite, even your life
  is tender—
I lift the book and blow you into
  the dazzling void.

ALLEN GINSBERG

Don't kill him!
  the fly it wrings its hands,
    its feet.

ISSA

A branch shorn of leaves
a crow perching on it—
this autumn eve.

BASHO

IN A STATION OF THE METRO

The apparition of these faces
    in the crowd;
Petals on a wet, black bough.

EZRA POUND

Men argue, nature acts.

VOLTAIRE

When it blows,
The mountain wind is
    boisterous,
But when it blows not,
It simply blows not.

EMILY BRONTË

Sitting quietly, doing nothing, spring comes, and the grass grows by itself.

ZEN SAYING

Of course the Dharma-body of the Buddha was the hedge at the bottom of the garden. At the same time, and no less obviously, it was these flowers, it was anything that I—or rather the blessed Not-I— cared to look at.

ALDOUS HUXLEY

To see a World in a grain of sand,
And a Heaven in a wild flower,
Hold infinity in the palm of your
      hand,
And eternity in an hour.

WILLIAM BLAKE

To make a prairie it takes
   a clover and one bee,
One clover, and a bee,
And revery.
The revery alone will do,
If bees are few.

EMILY DICKINSON

Basho

Though not a Zen monk, Matsuo Basho (1644–1694), Japan's greatest poet and one of the great lyric poets in any language, elevated the haiku form to the level of art and infused it with the spirit of Zen and the Tao. "Learn the rules well, and then forget them," he advised his students. He also told them: "Go to the pine if you want to learn about the pine, or to the bamboo if you want to learn about the bamboo. And in so doing you must let go of your subjective preoccupation with yourself. . . . Your poetry arises by itself when you and the object have become one."

Basho revered nature, children, the moon. He found the universe in the smallest detail, which he saw with the innocent eye of a child, and spent his later years on often lonely pilgrimages across Japan. "Old Pond," his best-known haiku, has been interpreted as a kind of koan, the frog disclosing the final meaning of reality:

> *Old pond,*
> *frog jumps in—*
> *plop.*

When a fish swims, it swims on and on, and there is no end to the water. When a bird flies, it flies on and on, and there is no end to the sky. There was never a fish that swam out of the water, or a bird that flew out of the sky. When they need a little water or sky, they use just a little; when they need a lot, they use a lot. Thus they use all of it at every moment, and in every place they have perfect freedom.

DOGEN

Consider the lilies of the field, how they grow; they toil not, neither do they spin:

And yet I say unto you, That even Solomon in all his glory was not arrayed like one of these.

MATTHEW 6:28–29

Each portion of matter may be conceived of as a garden full of plants, and as a pond full of fishes. But each branch of the plant, each member of the animal, each drop of its humors, is also such a garden or such a pond.

LEIBNIZ

As is the human body,
   so is the cosmic body.
As is the human mind,
   so is the cosmic mind.
As is the microcosm,
   so is the macrocosm.
As is the atom,
   so is the universe.

THE UPANISHADS

Butter tea and wind pictures, the Crystal Mountain, and blue sheep dancing on the snow—it's quite enough!

Have you seen the snow leopard? No! Isn't that wonderful?

PETER MATTHIESSEN

Earth's crammed with heaven,
And every common bush afire
　　with God:
But only he who sees takes off
　　his shoes.

ELIZABETH BARRETT BROWNING

Everything is holy!
everybody's holy!
everywhere is holy!
everyday is in eternity!
Everyman's an angel!

ALLEN GINSBERG

Goodnight stars.
Goodnight air.

MARGARET WISE BROWN

A heavy snowfall disappears into the sea. What silence!

FOLK ZEN SAYING

Knock on the sky and listen to the sound!

ZEN SAYING

This magnificent butterfly finds a little heap of dirt and sits still on it; but man will never on his heap of mud keep still . . .

JOSEPH CONRAD

With the evening breeze
the water laps
against the heron's legs.

BUSON

One real world is enough.

SANTAYANA

Each molecule preaches
    perfect law,

Each moment chants true
    sutra:

The most fleeting thought
    is timeless,

A single hair's enough to
    stir the sea.

SHUTAKU

Modern Physics

Found in the beginning of the Heart Sutra, a Buddhist work that holds a preeminent place in Zen, are the words:

> *Form is no different from emptiness.*
> *Emptiness is no different from form.*
> *Form is precisely emptiness,*
> *emptiness is precisely form.*

Two thousand years later, Western physicists agree.

Science's concept of the universe was changed irrevocably by quantum mechanics and Einstein's theory of relativity which questioned the separate identity of energy and matter. Our comfortable ideas of a universe made up of solid little bits of matter behaving in logical ways have been exploded.

A particle is not a separate entity but a set of relationships. The world is an interconnected tissue of events, a dynamic unbroken whole. Scientists are no longer observers but participants. And physics and mysticism converge in striking parallels, leading back full circle:

"A powerful awareness lies dormant in these discoveries [of modern physics]: an awareness of the hitherto-unsuspected powers of the mind to mold 'reality,' rather than the other way around. In this sense the philosophy of physics is becoming indistinguishable from the philosophy of Buddhism, which is the philosophy of enlightenment."

GARY ZUKOV, *THE DANCING WU-LI MASTERS*

Things derive their being and nature by mutual dependence and are nothing in themselves.

NAGARJUNA,
second-century Buddhist philosopher

An elementary particle is not an independently existing, unanalyzable entity. It is, in essence, a set of relationships that reach outward to other things.

H.P. STAPP,
twentieth-century physicist

A page from a journal of modern experimental physics will be as mysterious to the uninitiated as a Tibetan mandala. Both are records of inquiries into the nature of the universe.

FRITJOF CAPRA

I'm astounded by people who want to "know" the universe when it's hard enough to find your way around Chinatown.

WOODY ALLEN

If we ask, for instance, whether the position of the electron remains the same, we must say "no"; if we ask whether the electron's position changes with time, we must say "no"; if we ask whether the electron is at rest, we must say "no"; if we ask whether it is in motion, we must say "no."

J. ROBERT OPPENHEIMER

The "silly question" is the first intimation of some totally new development.

ALFRED NORTH WHITEHEAD

The world is charged with
the grandeur of God.

GERARD MANLEY HOPKINS

The Buddha, the Godhead, resides quite as comfortably in the circuits of a digital computer or the gears of a cycle transmission as he does at the top of a mountain or in the petals of a flower. To think otherwise is to demean the Buddha—which is to demean oneself.

ROBERT M. PIRSIG

With all your science can you tell how it is, and whence it is, that light comes into the soul?

THOREAU

To ask the hard
question is simple.

W.H. AUDEN

What is your original face before your mother and father were born?

ZEN KOAN

It is as hard to see one's self as to look backwards without turning around.

THOREAU

Search back into your own vision— think back to the mind that thinks. Who is it?

WU-MEN

What is troubling us is the tendency to believe that the mind is like a little man within.

LUDWIG WITTGENSTEIN

Great Faith.
Great Doubt.
Great Effort.

THE THREE QUALITIES NECESSARY
FOR TRAINING

Kung Yi-tsu was famous for his strength. King Hsüan of Chou went to call on him with full ceremony, but when he got there, he found that Kung was a weakling. The king asked, "How strong are you?" Kung replied, "I can break the waist of a spring insect, I can bear the wing of an autumn cicada." The king flushed and said, "I'm strong enough to tear apart rhinoceros hide and drag nine oxen by the tail—yet I still lament my weakness. How can it be that you are so famous for strength?" Kung replied, "My fame is not for having such strength, it is for being able to use such strength."

A monk brought two potted plants to his Master. "Drop it," ordered the Master. The monk dropped one pot. "Drop it," again ordered the Master. The monk let the second pot go. "Drop it," now roared the Master. The monk stammered: "But I have nothing to drop." The Master nodded. "Then take it away."

ZEN PARABLE

Get rid of the self and act from the Self!

ZEN SAYING

The true value of a
human being can be
found in the degree to
which he has attained
liberation from the self.

ALBERT EINSTEIN

The Zen Master said,
"Who binds you?"
    The seeker of liberty
said, "No one binds me."
    The Zen Master said,
"Then why seek liberation?"

ZEN MONDO

D.T. Suzuki

In a historic feat of cultural transmission, the lay Zen student and scholar Daisetz Teitaro Suzuki (1870–1966) introduced generations of Westerners to Zen Buddhism. Beginning with a translation of *Ashvagosha's Discourse on the Awakening of Faith in the Mahayana*, D.T. Suzuki published dozens of books and articles that clarified Zen for Westerners. Avoiding both historical and philosophical analysis, he presented Zen as "a wafting cloud in the sky. No screw fastens it, no string holds it. . . ."

By the 1950s, when he settled in New York and taught classes at Columbia to the likes of Erich Fromm, John Cage, Karen Horney and others, Suzuki had caught the popular imagination. His books, direct, humorous, grounded in experience and scholarship, were turning up in paperback. He was profiled in *The New Yorker* and interviewed on television. In Thomas Merton's words, "In meeting him one seemed to meet that 'True Man of No Title' that the Zen Masters speak of. And of course this is the man one really wants to meet."

"Zen is the ultimate fact of all philosophy," wrote Suzuki. "That final psychic fact that takes place when religious consciousness is heightened to extremity. . . in Buddhists, in Christians, in philosophers."

Zen in its essence is the art of seeing into the nature of one's being, and it points the way from bondage to freedom.

D.T. SUZUKI

The purpose of Zen is the perfection of character.

YAMADA ROSHI

Know thyself? If I knew myself, I'd run away.

GOETHE

Whoever knows himself knows God.

MUHAMMAD

The most terrifying thing is to accept oneself completely.

CARL JUNG

If you gaze for long into the abyss, the abyss also gazes into you.

NIETZSCHE

The more we understand individual things, the more we understand God.

SPINOZA

One day Chao-chou fell down in the snow, and called out, "Help me up! Help me up!" A monk came and lay down beside him. Chao-chou got up and went away.

ZEN KOAN

WITHOUT

the silence
of nature
within

the power within.
the power

without.

the path is whatever passes—no
end in itself.

the end is,
grace—ease—

healing,
not saving.

singing
the proof

the proof of the power within.

GARY SNYDER

Who *is* the Potter, pray, and who the Pot?

THE RUBÁIYÁT OF OMAR KHAYYÁM

He who knows others is
   wise.

He who knows himself is
   enlightened.

TAO TE CHING

Man only plays when in the full meaning of the word he is a man, and he is only completely a man when he plays.

FRIEDRICH VON SCHILLER

Ah but I was so much older then;
I'm younger than that now.

BOB DYLAN

A Great Fool

Daigu Ryokan (literally, "Great Fool") is one of the most beloved figures in Japanese folk tradition. A Zen poet-monk, he loved children and playing a happy game of ball, which he called "the highest form of Zen."

After receiving the seal of enlightenment from his Soto Master, Ryokan (1758–1831) chose not to take students but to emulate the monks of old, living in solitude as a mountain hermit and relying on alms for sustenance. He endured bitter periods of poverty, yet never lost his extraordinary innocence and loving heart. When a burglar ransacked his hut after discovering nothing of value, Ryokan wrote a haiku:

The thief left it there
there in the window—
the shining moon.

Ryokan wrote poetry that is among the most beautiful in Zen literature. But he also left behind his "Great Fool's" essence, as in the popular story about a game of hide-and-seek. As it grew dark, the children seeking Ryokan went home, but the monk continued hiding. The next morning a farmer found Ryokan behind a haystack. "Hush," he said, "or the children will find me!"

I am a writer who came from a sheltered life. A sheltered life can be a daring life as well. For all serious daring starts from within.

Eudora Welty

Can you walk on water? You have done no better than a straw. Can you fly in the air? You have done no better than a bluebottle. Conquer your heart; then you may become somebody.

ANSARI OF HERAT

How many cares one loses when one decides not to be something but to be someone.

COCO CHANEL

The self says, I am;
The heart says, I am less;
The spirit says, you are
  nothing.

THEODORE ROETHKE

That which transcends both the self and the other, that's what my teaching is about. Let me prove this to you: While everyone is turned this way to hear me, out back there may be sparrows chirping, human voices calling, or the sighing of the wind. But, without your consciously trying to hear them, each of those sounds comes to you clearly recognized and distinguished. It's not *you* doing the hearing, so it's not a matter of the self. But since no one else does your hearing for you, you couldn't call it the other! When you listen this way with the Unborn Buddha-mind—you transcend whatever there is.

BANKEI

see without looking, hear without listening, breathe without asking.

W.H. AUDEN

Life is what happens
to you while you're busy
making other plans.

JOHN LENNON

When making your choice in life, do not neglect to live.

SAMUEL JOHNSON

People say that what we're all seeking is a meaning for life. . . . I think that what we're really seeking is an experience of being alive, so that our life experiences on the purely physical plane will have resonance within our innermost being and reality, so that we can actually feel the rapture of being alive.

JOSEPH CAMPBELL

The aim of life is to live, and to live means to be aware, joyously, drunkenly, serenely, divinely aware.

HENRY MILLER

Dharma Bums

It was the Fifties. Zen was suddenly happening. A handful of Americans were off to postwar Japan and entering monasteries. D.T. Suzuki was giving his classes at Columbia, Nyogen Senzaki's floating zendo in Los Angeles was attracting a following. Zen seemed to be everywhere.

But no one embodied America's first infatuation with Zen like the Beats—Jack Kerouac, Gary Snyder, Allen Ginsberg, Philip Whalen, Lew Welch, and other artists and writers. They were "Zen Lunatics," as Kerouac called them in *The Dharma Bums*, his 1958 novel of Japhy Ryder (Gary Snyder) and the West Coast milieu of Buddhism and poetry.

Kerouac adopted Buddhism's first noble truth—*all life is suffering*—as the philosophic underpinning of his writing. Ginsberg found in the idea of satori an explanation for a powerful vision he had once experienced. Snyder first heard of Zen in college and would spend close to a decade refining his study in Japan—sharing, before he left, these words that Kerouac broadcast in *Dharma Bums*:

"I see. . . a great rucksack revolution, thousands or even millions of young Americans wandering around with rucksacks, going up to mountains to pray, making children laugh, and old men glad, making young girls happy, and old girls happier, all of 'em Zen lunatics who go about writing poems that happen to appear in their heads for no reason. . . . wild gangs of pure holy men getting together to drink and talk and pray."

Soon I was running across the moor to a distant part of the coast of Kintyre. . . . I felt I was running back to all the primitive joy that my season had destroyed. . . . The gulls were crying overhead and a herd of wild goats were silhouetted against the headland. I could barely distinguish slippery rock from heathery turf or bog, yet my feet did not slip or grow weary now—they had new life and confidence. I ran in a frenzy of speed, drawn on by an unseen force. The sun sank, setting the forest ablaze, and turning the sky to dull smoke. Then tiredness came on and. . .I rolled down a heather-topped bank and lay there happily exhausted.

ROGER BANNISTER

How refreshing, the whinny
of a packhorse unloaded of
everything!

ZEN SAYING

Later, he remembered certain moments in which the power of *this* moment was already contained, as in a seed. He thought of the hour in that other southern garden (Capri) when the call of a bird did not, so to speak, break off at the edge of his body, but was simultaneously outside and in his innermost being, uniting both into one uninterrupted space in which, mysteriously protected, only one single place of purest, deepest consciousness remained. On that occasion he had closed his eyes . . . and the Infinite passed into him from all sides, so intimately that he believed he could feel the stars which had in the meantime appeared, gently reposing within his breast.

RILKE

Thus shall ye think of all
     this fleeting world:
A star at dawn, a bubble in
     a stream;
A flash of lightning in a
     summer cloud,
A flickering lamp, a
     phantom, and a dream.

THE BUDDHA

When I dance, I dance; when I sleep, I sleep; yes, and when I walk alone in a beautiful orchard, if my thoughts drift to far-off matters for some part of the time, for some other part I lead them back again to the walk, the orchard, to the sweetness of this solitude, to myself.

MONTAIGNE

Right now a moment of time is fleeting by! Capture its reality in paint! To do that we must put all else out of our minds. We must become that moment, make ourselves a sensitive recording plate . . . give the image of what we actually see, forgetting everything that has been seen before our time.

PAUL CÉZANNE

The story is told that one of the elders lay dying in Scete, and the brethren surrounded his bed, dressed him in the shroud and began to weep. But the elder opened his eyes and laughed. He laughed another time, and then a third time. When the brethren saw this, they asked him, saying: "Tell us, Father, why are you laughing while we weep?" He said to them: "I laughed the first time because you fear death. I laughed the second time because you are not ready for death. And the third time I laughed because from labors I go to my rest." As soon as he had said this, he closed his eyes and died.

DESERT HERMIT ZEN

God be in my head
And in my understanding;
God be in mine eyes
And in my looking;
God be in my mouth
And in my speaking;
God be in my heart
And in my thinking;
God be at my end
And at my departing.

SARUM PRIMER

Death Poetry

Traditionally, a Zen Master would write a poem when he was about to die. Charged with his spirit, the Master's poem served both as a summation of life and as a parting gift to inspire his disciples.

Some chastise gently:

> *Coming and going, life and death:*
> *A thousand hamlets, a million houses.*
> *Don't you get the point?*
> *Moon in the water, blossom in the sky.*
>   GIZAN

Some say a relieved goodbye after a hard life:

> *Finally out of reach—*
> *No bondage, no dependency.*
> *How calm the ocean,*
> *Towering the void.*
>   TESSHO

Some merely shrug:

> *Life as we*
> *Find it—death too.*
> *A parting poem?*
> *Why insist?*
>> TA-HUI TSUNG-KAO

And some exult:

> *Four and fifty years*
> *I've hung the sky with stars.*
> *Now I leap through—*
> *What shattering!*
>> DOGEN

BRAHMA

If the red slayer think he slays
Or if the slain think he is slain
They know not well the subtle ways
I keep, and pass, and turn again.

EMERSON

One world at a time.

THOREAU,
when asked about the hereafter

Get up and do something useful, the work is part of the koan!

HAKUIN

Chop wood, carry water.

ZEN SAYING

Lift the stone and you will find me; cleave the wood and I am there.

JESUS

A monk asked Chao-chou, "I have just entered the monastery: please give me some guidance."

Chao-chou said, "Have you eaten your rice gruel?"

The monk said, "Yes, I've eaten."

Chao-chou said, "Then go wash your bowl."

ZEN MONDO

Dogen

While Zen was still in its infancy in Japan, a gifted monk named Dogen (1200–1253) made the hazardous voyage to China to seek the Way. Although he would meet many Masters and receive a certificate of enlightenment, it was perhaps the old Chinese monastery cook, visiting the newly landed ship to buy Japanese mushrooms, who gave Dogen his purest taste of Zen. Dogen asked the cook to stay and talk, but he begged off, saying he must get back to his duties. When the surprised Dogen asked him why he didn't practice zazen and leave the food to others, the old cook scoffed. Did the ignorant Japanese monk know nothing of the spirit of Buddhism?

Dogen, who would go on to become not only

the most important Soto Zen master in Japan but one of humankind's great religious spirits, never forgot the lessons of the cook—that work is fundamentally important to Zen and that enlightenment can be found in even the most ordinary places and acts. "Each and every extraordinary activity," he wrote, "is simply having rice."

1. Out of clutter, find simplicity.

2. From discord, find harmony.

3. In the middle of difficulty
   lies opportunity.

ALBERT EINSTEIN,
three rules of work

Zen is not some kind of excitement, but concentration on our usual everyday routine.

SHUNRYU SUZUKI

We have to understand that the world can only be grasped by action, not by contemplation. The hand is more important than the eye. . . . The hand is the cutting edge of the mind.

JACOB BRONOWSKI

Work is love made visible. And if you cannot work with love but only with distaste, it is better that you should leave your work and sit at the gate of the temple and take alms of those who work with joy.

KAHLIL GIBRAN

So the thing to do when working on a motorcycle, as in any other task, is to cultivate the peace of mind which does not separate one's self from one's surroundings. When that is done successfully, then everything else follows naturally. Peace of mind produces right values, right values produce right thoughts. Right thoughts produce right actions and right actions produce work which will be a material reflection for others to see of the serenity at the center of it all.

ROBERT M. PIRSIG

He did each single thing
as if he did nothing else.

CHARLES DICKENS

That is happiness: to be dissolved into something complete and great.

WILLA CATHER

A monk asked Ts'ui-wei about the meaning of Buddhism. Ts'ui-wei answered: "Wait until there is no one around, and I will tell you." Some time later the monk approached Ts'ui-wei again, saying: "There is nobody here now. Please answer me." Ts'ui-wei led him out into the garden and went over to the bamboo grove, saying nothing. Still the monk did not understand, so at last Ts'ui-wei said: "Here is a tall bamboo; there is a short one!"

ZEN PARABLE

Zen and the Art of Painting and Calligraphy

One of the most highly regarded art forms in East Asia, calligraphy is considerably older than Zen, and not all outstanding examples are Zen-related. But from its beginnings Zen found a natural affinity with the demanding, spontaneous quality of the ink brush. Using the heightened powers of concentration gained by meditation, Zen practitioners were capable of the most creative expression in calligraphy. As the Chinese Zen poet Huang T'ing-chien noticed, calligraphy changed after attaining enlightenment, the clear, sharp lines possessed of a new inner vitality.

Ink painting is Zen art at its highest expression. Zen painters demonstrate a profound communion with nature. The painter approaches his canvas as part of his practice, as contemplation, "empty canvas, blank mind." Beauty is a secondary consideration, with asymmetry, rather than balance, the aim. And empty space is as real as objects and solids; what is left out is as important as what is left in. Using a loaded ink brush on white silk or rice paper requires the utmost control. The first stroke is the final stroke; there can be no subsequent correction. Full of silence, timelessness and transparency, the paintings hint at an absolute reality beyond which nothing can be said. They are, in the words of one Western art historian, "ciphers of transcendence."

Draw bamboos for ten years, become a bamboo, then forget all about bamboos when you are drawing.

GEORGES DUTHUIT,
on painting in China

How can you think and hit at the same time?

Yogi Berra

The prayer of the monk is not perfect until he no longer recognizes himself or the fact that he is praying.

St. Anthony

As soon as my bull came out I went up to it, and at the third pass heard the howl of the multitude rising to their feet. What had I done? All at once I forgot the public, the other bullfighters, myself, and even the bull; I began to fight as I had so often by myself at night in the corrals and pastures. . . . They say that my passes with the cape and my work with the muleta that afternoon were a revelation of the art of bullfighting. I don't know. I simply fought without a thought outside my own faith in what I was doing. With the last bull I succeeded for the first time in my life in delivering myself body and soul to the pure joy of fighting.

JUAN BELMONTE

I believe a work of grass
is no less than the
journey-work of the stars.

WALT WHITMAN

If you study Japanese art, you see a man who is undoubtedly wise, philosophic, and intelligent, who spends his time how? In studying the distance between the earth and the moon? No. In studying the policy of Bismarck? No. He studies a single blade of grass. But this blade of grass leads him to draw every plant and then the seasons, the wide aspects of the countryside, then animals, then the human figure. So he passes his life, and life is too short to do the whole.

VINCENT VAN GOGH

—Children, one earthly Thing
truly experienced, even once,
     is enough for a lifetime.

RILKE

When you understand one thing through and through, you understand everything.

Shunryu Suzuki

What is the color of wind?

ZEN KOAN

The world is its own magic.

SHUNRYU SUZUKI

The mystical is not *how* the world is, but *that* it is.

LUDWIG WITTGENSTEIN

No ideas but in things.

WILLIAM CARLOS WILLIAMS

After we came out of the church, we stood talking for some time together of Bishop Berkeley's ingenious sophistry to prove the non-existence of matter, and that everything in the universe is merely ideal. I observed that though we are satisfied his doctrine is not true, it is impossible to refute it. I shall never forget the alacrity with which Johnson answered, striking his foot with mighty force against a large stone, "I refute it *thus*!"

BOSWELL,
Life of Samuel Johnson

Fa-yen, a Chinese Zen teacher, overheard four monks arguing about subjectivity and objectivity. He joined them and said: "There is a big stone. Do you consider it to be inside or outside your mind?"

One of the monks replied: "From the Buddhist viewpoint everything is an objectification of mind, so I would say that the stone is inside my mind."

"Your head must feel very heavy," observed Fa-yen, "if you are carrying around a stone like that in your mind."

ZEN STORY

We are here and it is now. Further than that, all human knowledge is moonshine.

H.L. MENCKEN

This is this.

THE DEER HUNTER

◪

Only *This, This!*

SOEN

I like reality. It tastes of bread.

JEAN ANOUILH

A painting of a rice cake does not satisfy hunger.

ANCIENT SAYING

When you ride in a boat and watch the shore, you might assume that the shore is moving. But when you keep your eyes closely on the boat, you can see that the boat moves. Similarly, if you examine many things with a confused mind, you might suppose that your mind and nature are permanent. But when you practice intimately and return to where you are, it will be clear that there is nothing that has unchanging self.

DOGEN

Empty-handed, holding
     a hoe,
Walking, riding a water
     buffalo.
Man is crossing a bridge;
The bridge but not the river
     flows.

MAHASATTVA FU

A painting by Van Gogh. A pair of rough peasant shoes, nothing else. Actually the painting represents nothing. But as to what *is* in that picture, you are immediately alone with it as though you yourself were making your way wearily homeward with your hoe on an evening in late fall after the last potato fires have died down. What *is* here? The canvas? The brush strokes? The spots of color?

MARTIN HEIDEGGER

When you meet a master
        swordsman,
show him your sword.
When you meet a man who is
        not a poet,
do not show him your poem.

LIN-CHI

Two monks were arguing about the temple flag waving in the wind. One said, "The flag moves." The other said, "The wind moves." They argued back and forth but could not agree. Hui-neng, the Sixth Patriarch, said: "Gentlemen! It is not the flag that moves. It is not the wind that moves. It is your mind that moves." The two monks were struck with awe.

ZEN KOAN

The river is moving.
The blackbird must be flying.

WALLACE STEVENS

Zen in the Art of Archery and Swordsmanship

In his classic account, *Zen in the Art of Archery*, the German philosopher Eugen Herrigal sought Zen's marrow in the training of an archer—to discover where art becomes artless, shooting becomes not-shooting, and the archer becomes the target. "'I'm afraid I don't understand anything more at all,' I answered, 'even the simplest things have got in a muddle. Is it "I" who draw the bow, or is it the bow that draws me? . . . Do "I" hit the goal or does the goal hit me? . . . Bow, arrow, goal and ego, all melt into one another, so that I can no longer separate them. And even the need to separate has gone. For as soon as I take the bow and shoot, everything becomes so clear and straightforward and ridiculously simple . . . 'Now at last,' the Master broke in, 'the bow-string has cut right through you.'"

When pursued in the spirit of Zen, fencing, like archery, becomes a spiritual discipline. Zen Masters fence, and adepts of *kendo*—Japanese fencing— often train in Zen. It is another way of pursuing *mushin*, or "no-mindness." As the swordsman transcends the limits of his technique, putting aside all notions of displaying skill or winning a contest, the sword and the swordsman become one. Thoughts and feelings drop away as the swordsman returns to his "original mind."

If you direct your mind toward the bodily movements of your opponent, your mind will be taken by the bodily movements of your opponent. If you direct your mind toward your opponent's sword, it will be taken by the sword. If you direct your mind toward trying to strike your opponent, it will be taken by waiting to strike. If you direct your mind toward your own sword, it will be taken by your sword. If you direct it toward not being struck, it will be taken by the desire not to be struck. If you direct it toward your opponent's attitude, it will be taken by his attitude. In short, there is nowhere to direct your mind.

TAKUAN

Be master of mind rather than mastered by mind.

ZEN SAYING

Should you desire the great tranquillity, prepare to sweat white beads.

HAKUIN

A condition of complete simplicity
(Costing not less than everything)

T.S. ELIOT

The reason angels can fly is that they take themselves so lightly.

G.K. CHESTERTON

Must it be?
It must be.

BEETHOVEN

I can't go on.
You must go on.
I'll go on.

SAMUEL BECKETT

When the way comes
to an end, then change—
having changed, you
pass through.

I CHING

It is like a water buffalo passing through a window. Its head, horns and four legs all pass through. Why can't its tail pass through, too?

ZEN KOAN

And do not change. Do not divert your love from visible things. But go on loving what is good, simple and ordinary; animals and things and flowers, and keep the balance true.

RILKE

Knock,
And He'll open the door.

Vanish,
And He'll make you shine like the sun.

Fall,
And He'll raise you to the heavens.

Become nothing,
And He'll turn you into everything!

RUMI

Everything is based on mind, is led by mind, is fashioned by mind. If you speak and act with a polluted mind, suffering will follow you, as the wheels of the oxcart follow the footsteps of the ox. Everything is based on mind, is led by mind, is fashioned by mind. If you speak and act with a pure mind, happiness will follow you, as a shadow clings to a form.

THE BUDDHA

There is nothing either good or bad but thinking makes it so.

SHAKESPEARE

When I'm in this state everything is pure, vividly clear. I'm in a cocoon of concentration. And if I can put myself into that cocoon, I'm invincible. . . . I'm living fully in the present. I'm absolutely engaged, *involved* in what I'm doing. . . . It comes and it goes, and the pure fact that you are out on the first tee of a tournament and say, "I must concentrate today," is no good. It won't work.

TONY JACKLIN

Pat Fischer, the Redskin cornerback, told the reporters after the game that the ball seemed to jump over his hands as he went for it. When we studied the game film that week, it *did* look as if the ball kind of jumped over his hands into Gene's. Some of the guys said it was the wind . . . [but] our sense of the pass was so clear and our *intention* so strong that the ball was bound to get there, come wind, cornerbacks, hell, or high water.

JOHN BRODIE

It is not the same to talk of bulls as to be in the bullring.

SPANISH PROVERB

We try to evade the question [of existence] with property, prestige, power, production, fun, and, ultimately, by trying to forget that we—that I—exist. No matter how often he *thinks* of God or goes to church, or how much he believes in religious ideas, if he, the whole man, is deaf to the question of existence, if he does not have an answer to it, he is marking time, and he lives and dies like one of the million things he produces. He *thinks* of God, instead of *experiencing* God.

ERICH FROMM

If people ask me what Zen is like, I will say that it is like learning the art of burglary. The son of a burglar saw his father growing older and thought: "If he is unable to carry out his profession, who will be the breadwinner of this family? I must learn the trade." One night the father took the son to a big house, broke through the fence, entered the house, and opening one of the large chests, told the son to go in and pick out the clothing. As soon as he got into it, the lid was dropped and the lock securely applied. The father now came out to the courtyard, and loudly knocking at the door woke up the whole family, whereas he himself quietly slipped away. The residents got up and lighted candles, but found that the burglars had already gone. The whole time, the son remained in the chest, and thought of his cruel father. Then a fine idea flashed upon him. He made a noise like the gnawing of a rat. When the lid was unlocked, out came the prisoner and fled. Noticing a well by the road, he picked up a large stone and threw it into the water. The pursuers gathered around the well trying to find the burglar drowning himself. By then, he was safely back in the house of his father, whom he blamed for his narrow escape. When the son told him about his adventures, the father remarked, "There, you have learned the art!"

D.T. SUZUKI

You can only find truth with logic if you have already found truth without it.

G.K. CHESTERTON

Pai-chang wished to send a monk to open a new monastery. He told his pupils that whoever answered a question most ably would be appointed. Placing a water jug on the ground, he asked: "Who can say what this is without calling its name?"

The head monk said: "No one can call it a wooden sandal."

Kuei-shan, the cooking monk, tipped over the jug with his foot and went out.

Pai-chang laughed and said: "The head monk loses."

And Kuei-shan became the Master of the new monastery.

ZEN MONDO

I AM THAT I AM.

OLD TESTAMENT KOAN

What is the sound of one hand clapping?

ZEN KOAN

Attachment is the great fabricator of illusions; reality can be attained only by someone who is detached.

SIMONE WEIL

Two monks were once traveling together down a muddy road. A heavy rain was falling. Coming around the bend, they met a lovely girl in a silk kimono and sash, unable to cross the intersection.

"Come on, girl," said the first monk. Lifting her in his arms, he carried her over the mud.

The second monk did not speak again until that night when they reached a lodging temple. Then he no longer could restrain himself. "We monks don't go near females," he said. "It is dangerous. Why did you do that?"

"I left the girl there," the first monk said. "Are you still carrying her?"

ZEN STORY

When an ordinary man attains knowledge, he is a sage; when a sage attains understanding, he is an ordinary man.

ZEN SAYING

Wealthy patrons invited Ikkyu to a banquet. Ikkyu arrived dressed in his beggar's robes. The host, not recognizing him, chased him away. Ikkyu went home, changed into his ceremonial robe of purple brocade, and returned. With great respect, he was received into the banquet room. There, he put his robe on the cushion, saying, "I expect you invited the robe since you showed me away a little while ago," and left.

ZEN STORY

Man's main task in life is to give birth to himself.

ERICH FROMM

You should study not only that you become a mother when your child is born, but also that you become a child.

DOGEN

Te-shan was sitting outside doing zazen. Lung-t'an asked him why he didn't go back home. Te-shan answered, "Because it's dark." Lung-t'an then lit a candle and handed it to him. As Te-shan was about to take it, Lung-t'an blew it out. Te-shan had a sudden realization, and bowed.

ZEN KOAN

You must concentrate upon and consecrate yourself wholly to each day, as though a fire were raging in your hair.

DESHIMARU

Just before she died, Gertrude Stein asked: "What is the answer?" No answer came. She laughed and said: "In that case what is the question?" Then she died.

Both speech and silence transgress.

ZEN SAYING

The Lotus Position

To practice Zen one must sit—and sit, to borrow from Dogen, like a great pine or a mountain, with a sense of dignity and grandeur.

Traditionally one sits in the full lotus position. The legs are crossed, with left foot on right thigh, right foot on the left. The spine curves forward slightly, letting the belly hang naturally while the posterior is pushed back for solid support—if you slump, you lose yourself. The head is up, chin is in, eyes are slightly open and cast down. Hands are placed in the lap and form a "cosmic mudra"—left hand on top of right, middle joints of middle fingers together and thumbs lightly touching to form an oval. The mudra must be kept with great care.

In the words of Shunryu Suzuki from *Zen Mind,*

Beginner's Mind: "When we cross our legs like this, even though we have a left leg and a right leg, they have become one. The position expresses the oneness of duality: not two, not one. This is the most important teaching: not two, and not one. Our body and mind are not two and not one. If you think your body and mind are two, that is wrong; if you think that they are one, that is also wrong. Our body and mind are both two *and* one."

Talking about Zen all the time is like looking for fish tracks in a dry riverbed.

WU-TZU

Our own life is the instrument with which we experiment with truth.

THICH NHAT HANH

One day Chuang-tzu and a friend were walking along a riverbank.

"How delightfully the fishes are enjoying themselves in the water!" Chuang-tzu exclaimed.

"You are not a fish," his friend said. "How do you know whether or not the fishes are enjoying themselves?"

"You are not me," Chuang-tzu said. "How do you know that I do not know that the fishes are enjoying themselves?"

TAOIST MONDO

"My feet are cold,"
one says, and the
legless man replies:
"So are mine.
So are mine."

KENTUCKY FOLKLORE

When you can do nothing, what can you do?

ZEN KOAN

Computers are useless. They can only give you answers.

PABLO PICASSO

Wisdom is like a mass of fire—it cannot be entered from any side.

■

Wisdom is like a clear cool pool—it can be entered from any side.

NAGARJUNA

A monk was anxious to learn Zen and said: "I have been newly initiated into the Brother-hood. Will you be gracious enough to show me the way to Zen?"

The Master said: "Do you hear the murmuring sound of the mountain stream?"

The monk said: "Yes, I do."

The Master said: "Here is the entrance."

ZEN MONDO

Meditation is not a means to an end. It is both the means and the end.

KRISHNAMURTI

The more you know
the less you understand.

TAO TE CHING

FURTHER READING

INTRODUCTORY AND GENERAL WORKS ON ZEN

AITKEN, ROBERT. *Taking the Path of Zen*. North Point.

DUMOULIN, HEINRICH. *Zen Buddhism: A History*. Vol. One: *India and China*. Vol. Two: *Japan and China*. Macmillan.

FIELDS, RICK. *How the Swans Came to the Lake*. Shambhala. ☑ A lively narrative of how Buddhism and Zen came to America.

KAPLEAU, ROSHI PHILLIP. *The Three Pillars of Zen*. Anchor Books. ☑ How-to, and how others did it.

ROSS, NANCY WILSON. *The World of Zen*. Vintage.

SUZUKI, D.T. *Essays in Zen Buddhism*. Grove Weidenfeld.
——. *An Introduction to Zen Buddhism*. Grove Weidenfeld. ☑ Suzuki Primer.

SUZUKI, SHUNRYU. *Zen Mind, Beginner's Mind*.
Weatherhill. ◪ A treasure.

WATTS, ALAN W. *The Spirit of Zen*. Vintage.
———. *The Way of Zen*. Vintage.

ORIGINAL WRITINGS AND SOURCES

AITKEN, ROBERT. *The Gateless Barrier*. North Point.
◪ A classic koan collection with instructive
commentary by an American Master.

CLEARY, THOMAS AND CLEARY, J.C. *The Blue Cliff Record*.
Shambhala. ◪ Another classic koan collection.

HASKEL, PETER. *Bankei Zen*. Grove Weidenfeld.
◪ Teachings of the unorthodox and greatly popular
seventeenth-century Japanese Master.

PRICE, A.F. AND MOU-LAM, WONG. *The Diamond Sutra
and The Platform Sutra of Hui-neng*. Shambhala.

REPS, PAUL. *Zen Flesh, Zen Bones*. Anchor.
☑ Wonderful stories.

SHIGEMATSU, SOIKU. *A Zen Forest*. Weatherhill.

TANAHASHI, KAZUAKI. *Moon in a Dewdrop*. North Point.
☑ Dogen's writings.

WATSON, BURTON. *The Zen Teachings of Master Lin-chi*.
Shambhala.

HAIKU, POETRY AND THE ARTS

AITKEN, ROBERT. *A Zen Wave*. Weatherhill.
☑ Basho's haiku.

BLYTH, R.H. *Haiku*. Hokuseido Press.
☑ An essential introduction.

STRYK, LUCIEN AND IKEMOTO, TAKASHI. *Zen Poems of
China and Japan*. Grove Weidenfeld.
——. *Zen Poetry*. Penguin.

Suzuki, D.T. *Zen and Japanese Culture.* Princeton University Press.

KINDRED SPIRITS

Blyth, R.H. *Zen in English Literature and Oriental Classics.* E.P. Dutton.

Capra, Fritjof. *The Tao of Physics.* Shambhala.

Herrigel, Eugen. *Zen in the Art of Archery.* Vintage.

Matthiessen, Peter. *Three Headed Dragon River.* Shambhala. ☑ The writer's search for enlightenment.

Merton, Thomas. *The Way of Chuang Tzu.* New Directions.

MITCHELL, STEPHEN. *The Enlightened Heart.*
HarperPerennial.
——. *The Enlightened Mind.* HarperPerennial.
——. *Tao Te Ching.* Harper & Row.

MURPHY, MICHAEL. *Golf in the Kingdom.* Arkana.
◾ Golf and mysticism.

PIRSIG, ROBERT M. *Zen and the Art of Motorcycle Maintenance.* Morrow.

WETERING, JANWILLEM VAN DE. *The Empty Mirror* and *A Glimpse of Nothingness.* Houghton Mifflin.
◾ Zen in Japan, then America, firsthand.

IN ADDITION

THOREAU, WALT WHITMAN, GARY SNYDER, RILKE, essays by EMERSON, JACK KEROUAC's *The Dharma Bums.*

CREDITS

DAVID SCHILLER IS A WRITER
WHO LIVES IN BROOKLYN, NEW YORK,
WITH HIS WIFE AND SON.